The INSIDE GUIDE

GLOBAL GEOGRAPHY

Exploring East and Southeast Asia's Geography

By Heather Smore

Cavendish Square

Published in 2026 by Cavendish Square Publishing, LLC
2544 Clinton Street Buffalo, NY 14224

Website: cavendishsq.com

Library of Congress Cataloging-in-Publication Data

Names: Smore, Heather, author.
Title: Exploring East and Southeast Asia's geography / Heather Smore.
Description: Buffalo, New York : Cavendish Square Publishing, [2026] | Series: The Inside Guide. Global geography | Includes index.
Identifiers: LCCN 2025000577 | ISBN 9781502674142 (lib. bdg.) | ISBN 9781502674135 (paperback) | ISBN 9781502674159 (ebook)
Subjects: LCSH: Nature–Effect of human beings on–Juvenile literature. | East Asia–Geography–Juvenile literature. | Southeast Asia–Geography–Juvenile literature.
Classification: LCC DS508.2 S555 2026 | DDC 915–dc23/eng/20250220
LC record available at https://lccn.loc.gov/2025000577

Editor: Katie Kawa
Designer: Deanna Lepovich

The photographs in this book are used by permission and through the courtesy of: Cover Chanunphat/Shutterstock.com; pp. 4, 7, 16 Peter Hermes Furian/Shutterstock.com; p. 6 Efired/Shutterstock.com; p. 8 (top) HelloRF Zcool/Shutterstock.com; p. 8 (bottom) BEST-BACKGROUNDS/Shutterstock.com; p. 9 Sean Pavone/Shutterstock.com; p. 10 ABCDstock/Shutterstock.com; p. 12 Tatiana_kashko_photo/Shutterstock.com; p. 13 Vixit/Shutterstock.com; p. 14 Mr. Aleksandr Lenkov/Shutterstock.com; p. 15 Mo Wu/Shutterstock.com; pp. 18 (top), 22 Guitar photographer/Shutterstock.com; p. 18 (bottom) Aleksandar Todorovic/Shutterstock.com; p. 19 ozerkizildag/Shutterstock.com; p. 20 Carl Schoeneich/Shutterstock.com; p. 21 Sean Hsu/Shutterstock.com; p. 24 Deni_Sugandi/Shutterstock.com; p. 25 WQ Photography/Shutterstock.com; p. 26 Richie Chan/Shutterstock.com; p. 27 satoriphoto/Shutterstock.com; p. 28 (top left) Sazid4/Shutterstock.com; p. 28 (top right) HobbitArt/Shutterstock.com; p. 28 (center) Oasis World/Shutterstock.com; p. 28 (bottom left) Extezy/Shutterstock.com; p. 28 (bottom right) MyPro/Shutterstock.com; p. 29 (left) i viewfinder/Shutterstock.com; p. 29 (right) dani daniar/Shutterstock.com.

CPSIA compliance information: Batch #CSCSQ26: For further information contact Cavendish Square Publishing LLC at 1-877-980-4450.

Printed in the United States of America

CONTENTS

The lands that make up East Asia are shown here. This region is home to many different landscapes, governments, and people.

THE LANDS OF EAST ASIA

Chapter One

Asia takes up around a third of Earth's entire surface. It's the largest continent on Earth, as well as the most populated. Because it's so large, it's often looked at in regions instead of as a whole. Two major regions of this continent are East Asia and Southeast Asia.

The geography of each region of Asia has had a major influence on the people who live there. In East Asia, which is home to more than 1.6 billion people, diverse landscapes have been shaping **cultures** for thousands of years.

Countries and Cities

East Asia includes some of the world's most **populous** and fascinating countries. The region is made up of the People's Republic of China (often simply called China), the Republic of China (more often called Taiwan), Japan, North Korea, South Korea, and Mongolia. It also includes Macau and Hong Kong, which are special regions within China.

> **Fast Fact**
>
> Asia covers more than 17 million square miles (44 million sq km) in area.

The major cities of East Asia are international hubs for trade, business,

Hong Kong, which is shown here, is one of the world's most important centers for trade and business.

and culture. They include Beijing and Shanghai in China, Tokyo in Japan, Seoul in South Korea, and Pyongyang in North Korea. These cities have developed their own unique **characteristics** based on their geography.

A Closer Look at China

The People's Republic of China is the largest country in East Asia. In fact, it's the largest country in all of Asia! China is home to mountains, deserts, and two major world rivers—the Huang He, or Yellow River, and the Yangtze.

China is broken up into divisions to make governing such a large country easier.

Fast Fact

Taiwan is a self-governed state that calls itself the Republic of China, but its independence is not recognized by many in the international community.

ASIA'S BORDERS

Asia is a continent with boundaries shaped by both land and sea. It is bordered by the Arctic Ocean to the north, the Pacific Ocean to the east, and the Indian Ocean to the south. To the west, it shares a border with Europe, part of which includes the Caucasus and Ural mountain ranges. However, this border is mostly determined by cultural differences, and there is some argument over where one continent ends and the other begins. Some geographers group Europe and Asia together as part of one supercontinent called Eurasia.

Asia is one of seven continents, which are shown here.

There are 22 provinces, which are like U.S. states. There are also other parts, such as Tibet, that have slightly more independence. In addition, the areas of Macau and Hong Kong are technically part of China, but

Beijing, which is shown here, is the capital of China.

they have their own governments, languages, and more.

The Korean Peninsula

Like other peninsulas, the Korean Peninsula is surrounded by water on three sides. It shares land borders with China and Russia. This peninsula is divided into two countries: North Korea and South Korea.

North Korea is a **dictatorship**, and its economy is based on **communism**. South Korea is more democratic and more economically developed than North Korea. Pyongyang is the capital of North Korea, and Seoul is the capital of South Korea. Despite their differences, these countries share many geographic features, including mountains and ocean coastlines.

The Korean Peninsula, which can be seen here, is surrounded by the Yellow Sea, the Korea Strait, and the Sea of Japan (also called the East Sea).

A Tour of Japan

Japan is an island country in the Pacific Ocean, off the coast of mainland Asia. Its geographic features have played a major part in shaping the Japanese way of life.

Japan is an **archipelago** made up of four main islands (Hokkaido, Honshu, Shikoku, and Kyushu) and thousands of tiny islands. Its mountainous landscape limits the land that can be used for farming and living. As a result, Japan's population is concentrated in small areas. Major cities in Japan include Tokyo, which is the capital of the country, Yokohama, and Osaka.

Nature is very important to the Japanese way of life. In the Shinto religion, which is practiced mainly in Japan, geographic features and natural objects, such as trees, mountains, streams, and rocks, are believed to contain spirits.

Fast Fact

In 2023, around 14 million people lived in the city of Tokyo, and around 20 million people from around the world visited the city.

Geographic features such as mountains have played a major part in construction projects throughout history. For example, parts of the Great Wall of China (*shown here*) were built over and through mountain ranges as a way to protect China from invaders.

MOUNTAINS, DESERTS, AND RIVERS

Chapter Two

The geography of East Asia has affected how people live, work, and travel in this region since the first groups began to settle there. Its extreme landscapes, such as mountain peaks and vast deserts, have kept certain areas isolated and seemingly frozen in time. On the other hand, its rivers and valleys have supported civilizations throughout history and allowed those civilizations to grow food, trade with other regions, and flourish.

The Roof of the World

The largest and highest plateau in the world—the Tibetan Plateau—is in East Asia. It is sometimes called the "Roof of the World." A plateau is a large area of land with raised sides and a level top, and this plateau reaches heights of more than 15,000 feet (4,572 m).

The Tibetan Plateau includes the entire region of Tibet in China, as well as other Chinese provinces. It is the starting place for a number of major rivers, and its glaciers contain large amounts of frozen water. However, climate change is causing these glaciers to shrink, which could cause flooding.

The Tibetan Plateau (*shown here*) is sometimes called the "Third Pole" because the only parts of the world with more water in the form of ice are the North and South Poles.

Mountain Ranges

Mountain ranges are found throughout East Asia. The Kunlun Mountains, which run through China and Tibet, make up one of the longest mountain chains in Asia. The mountains have a cold, windy climate all year long. Except for some **Indigenous** groups, few people live in the Kunlun Mountains.

Fast Fact

Mount Everest is located on the border between Nepal and China. It's technically located in both of those countries.

EARTHQUAKES AND TSUNAMIS

East and Southeast Asia are areas with a lot of geologic activity, which means a lot is happening just under Earth's surface. This activity is caused by large pieces of Earth's crust, called plates, crashing into each other. This can cause earthquakes. If an earthquake happens under an ocean, it can cause a **tsunami**. Tokyo frequently experiences earthquakes. In 2011, a huge earthquake hit Tokyo. It was a 9.0 on a scale of 10. The earthquake and the tsunami it caused resulted in the deaths of nearly 20,000 people. In 2004, an earthquake and tsunami that were centered in Indonesia killed around 228,000 people.

Fast Fact

Mount Fuji, which is the tallest mountain in Japan, is also an active volcano!

The Himalayas are one of the most famous geographic features in the world. These mountains form a natural boundary between several countries,

Mount Everest reaches a height of 29,032 feet (8,849 m) above sea level. In 2023, 656 climbers reached the mountain's summit, or highest point.

including China, Nepal, and India. They separate the Tibetan Plateau from the Indian **subcontinent**. The highest mountain in the world, Mount Everest, is part of the Himalayas.

Deserts in East Asia

Although East Asia is one of the most populated regions on Earth, few people live in the region's desert areas. The Gobi Desert is located in both Mongolia and China. This desert has rocky, mountainous terrain, so it is not good for growing food. Furthermore, the climate is very cold, which causes people to stay away.

The Taklamakan Desert is the largest desert in China and one of the largest sandy deserts in

Fast Fact

The Taklamakan Desert is a major source of oil for China.

The Gobi Desert is one of the largest deserts in the world. Unlike the Taklamakan Desert, the Gobi Desert has few sandy areas and is mostly made up of rocky ground.

the world. Its climate is harsh; temperatures can be either extremely cold or extremely hot. As with the Gobi Desert, few people have braved the extremes to live there.

Important Waterways

Water makes it possible to plant crops, raise animals, and support societies. This is why, throughout history, civilizations have settled near water. China's earliest civilization settled along the Huang He, or Yellow River, which begins in the mountains of western China.

The Yangtze River is China's longest river and the third-largest river in the world. The river has allowed ships to carry goods throughout China. Shanghai, one of the country's most populous cities, is located at the mouth of the Yangtze River, where it empties into the East China Sea.

The Yellow River gets its name from the color of the silt, or tiny pieces of sand and clay, carried in the water. Its unique color can be seen here.

Shown here is a map of Southeast Asia, which includes many islands, as well as mainland nations.

Chapter Three

ON THE MAINLAND

East Asia's neighbor is Southeast Asia. It's located right under China and is made up of 11 countries, which are located on the mainland and on various islands. The mainland countries that make up this region are Vietnam, Cambodia, Laos, Thailand, Myanmar, Malaysia, and the **city-state** of Singapore. Although Singapore is an island, it is connected to Malaysia by bridges. Mainland Southeast Asia and the islands have very different cultural landscapes, and there is much to learn about each area.

Vietnamese Geography

To the south of China lies the nation of Vietnam. It borders the South China Sea and has two major rivers: the Mekong and the Red. The areas where the rivers meet the sea are called deltas. Most Vietnamese citizens live in the deltas because the land there is fertile. For example, Hanoi, Vietnam's capital city, is located in the Red River Delta.

> **Fast Fact**
> Southeast Asia encompasses around 5 million square miles (13 million sq km) of land and water together.

Vietnam is affected by monsoons, which are seasonal winds that result in wet spring and summer months and dry winter months. Flooding is

Rice is a staple of the Vietnamese diet, so rice fields called paddies can be seen all over the country. Terrace farming, which is shown here, allows Vietnamese farmers to create rice paddies even where the land is steep.

a major problem in Vietnam, especially when tropical storms hit the country.

The Lands of Laos and Cambodia

Laos is west of Vietnam. The Mekong River provides the Laotian people with transportation, water for farming, and food. Laotians also use it for electricity, called hydropower. This river is extremely important to the landlocked country. Most of the population lives along the river because it is too hard to travel through Laos's forests and mountains.

Cambodia is bordered by Laos, Vietnam, Thailand, and the Gulf of Thailand.

Like Vietnam, Cambodia often deals with flooding. Cambodians who live in areas that often flood have adapted by building wooden houses on stilts. This design keeps the house high off the ground and safe from flooding.

Central Cambodia is a low and flat plain. Phnom Penh, located in the southern part of the country, is Cambodia's major city. It is located where three rivers meet and is a major center of industry.

A Tour of Thailand

Thailand is at the center of mainland Southeast Asia. It is bordered by Myanmar, Cambodia, Laos, and the Gulf of Thailand. The lowest-lying areas of Thailand are at sea level, which creates swampy landscapes.

The Thai people have adapted to this landscape by turning the waterways into a means of transportation. The Chao Phraya River is important for carrying goods, fishing, and transportation. The Thai capital, Bangkok, is located at the mouth of this river. Bangkok has an extensive network of canals, called klongs, that run from the river and throughout the city. People use the canals to travel around Bangkok.

In Bangkok, boats travel up and down the canals, taking people to work, to their homes, and to markets to buy things. Some of these markets are on land, but many others, such as the one shown here, float on the water.

Myanmar and Malaysia

Thailand extends south down the Malay Peninsula. Myanmar also stretches down this peninsula. This country was formerly known as Burma, and it is the largest country in mainland Southeast Asia. The Yangon River is an important water source in Myanmar, and the country's largest city, Yangon, is located on its banks.

Fast Fact

The island of Borneo is divided between three countries: Malaysia, Brunei, and Indonesia. It's the third-largest island in the world!

The Malay Peninsula connects Thailand and Myanmar to Malaysia. Malaysia's geography is unique: The country is made of two areas of land that are separated by a body of water. The western portion, called Peninsular Malaysia, is on the Malay Peninsula. Across the South China Sea is East Malaysia. It's on the island of Borneo.

Fast Fact

Myanmar is the northernmost country in Southeast Asia. In addition to Thailand and Malaysia, it also borders Laos and China.

Shown here are limestone formations in Malaysia's Gunung Mulu National Park. This park contains many amazing geographic features, including one of the largest caves in the world.

THE CITY-STATE OF SINGAPORE

At the southern tip of the Malay Peninsula is a waterway called the Johor Strait. Across this waterway is Singapore, a city-state that is one of the biggest and busiest seaports in the world. Singapore was colonized by Great Britain in 1946 and then became part of Malaysia in 1963. It became independent in 1965. Today, Singapore is one of Southeast Asia's most economically developed areas. Many people live in the city, making it very crowded. However, even in this bustling city, people can find themselves surrounded by beautiful plants in the park known as the Gardens by the Bay.

The Gardens by the Bay were created to bring more natural beauty to the urban landscapes of Singapore.

Shown here is a temple, or holy building, in Indonesia. This Southeast Asian nation is the largest country in the world made up of one or more island chains.

ISLAND LIFE

Chapter Four

Islands are a major part of Southeast Asia. Although some mainland nations may have islands within their borders and Singapore is an island connected to the mainland by bridges, some Southeast Asian nations are made up entirely of islands. The countries of Indonesia, Brunei, Timor-Leste, and the Philippines are island nations and are not connected to the mainland of Southeast Asia.

The Islands of Indonesia

Indonesia is an island nation known for its natural beauty. It is located between the Indian Ocean and Pacific Ocean. Indonesia is part of the Malay Archipelago. It contains more than 17,000 islands that cover 3,200 miles (5,149.9 km) from east to west.

Fast Fact

The Indonesian island of Java has the largest population of any island on Earth. It is home to over 150 million people!

Only about 6,000 Indonesian islands are known to be inhabited, or settled by people. The country's population is scattered and divided among these islands. The major islands of Indonesia include

THE RING OF FIRE

Indonesia is home to hundreds of volcanoes. This is because of its location on what's known as the Ring of Fire. This is an area around the Pacific Ocean where large numbers of earthquakes and volcanic eruptions occur because of the movement of plates beneath Earth's surface. The Ring of Fire includes parts of North and South America, as well as parts of Asia and Oceania. Many areas of East and Southeast Asia are located on the Ring of Fire. For example, Japan is located there, which is the reason for its many earthquakes.

Shown here is a volcanic eruption in Indonesia.

Sumatra, Sulawesi, Kalimantan (part of the island of Borneo), Bali, and Java.

Another Archipelago

The Philippines is another major archipelago in Southeast Asia. It is made up of more than 7,100 islands. These islands are located between the Pacific Ocean and the South China Sea. Only about a third of the islands are inhabited.

The capital of the Philippines is Manila, which is located on Luzon—the largest island in the archipelago. Mindanao is the second-largest island in the Philippines by area. The Visayas are a group of islands within the Philippines that make up another major region of the country.

Fast Fact

Farming is an important part of the economy of the Philippines. Major crops include rice and coconuts.

The People of the Islands

The other two island nations of Southeast Asia share islands

The Philippines is an island nation of big cities, beautiful beaches, tropical forests, and impressive waterfalls, such as Hulugan Falls (*shown here*).

Shown here is a mosque, or Islamic gathering place, in Brunei. This small island nation is known for its high standard of living.

with larger countries. Brunei is an Islamic nation on the island of Borneo, which it shares with Malaysia and Indonesia. Timor-Leste, or East Timor, shares the island of Timor with Indonesia.

The people of these islands, like the people of Indonesia and the Philippines, use their ocean surroundings to their advantage. Fishing provides a source of income as well as food for many people, and people in this region have traveled by water to trade for centuries. Tourism in these countries is also tied to the water—people visit locations like Bali for the beautiful beaches and ocean views.

Fast Fact

Asia's population is growing, but land is limited. Many cities have turned to high-rise buildings for housing, building up instead of spreading out.

Geography and Culture

If you want to learn more about how a society developed, look at its surrounding geography. The geography of East and Southeast Asia has impacted the cultures that developed there from ancient times to today.

Over thousands of years, people in East and Southeast Asia learned how to use their geography to the best of their ability. Farmers focused on crops that grew well in warm, rainy climates. Settlements appeared along major rivers, which supported life, trade, and farming. While some areas have been isolated due to their geography, modern transportation has allowed more people than ever before to see these amazing places for themselves.

Today, people from all over the world travel to East and Southeast Asia to take in the beautiful sights, such as those of Ha Long Bay in Vietnam (*shown here*).

EAST AND SOUTHEAST ASIA BY THE NUMBERS

Largest Country (by Area)

China: 3.7 million square miles (9.6 million sq km)

Most Populated Country

China: 1.4 billion people

Smallest Country (by Area)

Singapore: 284 square miles (735 sq km)

Highest Point

Mount Everest: 29,032 feet (8,849 m) above sea level

Longest River

Yangtze (China): 3,915 miles (6,300 km)

THINK ABOUT IT!

1. Do you think geographic features that isolate a country from the rest of the world, such as mountains or oceans, are helpful for that country or harmful? Why?
2. What effect do you think Asia's growing population has on its geography?
3. Why do you think people have always chosen to live near water sources, even if they can cause dangerous flooding?
4. How might climate change affect East and Southeast Asia's geography in the future?

GLOSSARY

archipelago: A group of islands.

characteristic: A special quality that makes something or someone different from others.

city-state: A self-governing state made up of a city and surrounding lands.

communism: A social and economic system in which all property and goods are shared and there is common ownership.

culture: The beliefs and ways of life of a certain group of people.

dictatorship: A form of government in which a person rules a country with total power and often in a harmful way.

Indigenous: Relating to the earliest known inhabitants of a place.

populous: Having a large population.

subcontinent: A major part of a continent.

tsunami: A huge sea wave produced by the movement of the earth under water.

FIND OUT MORE

Books

Brink, Tracy Vonder. *Asia*. New York, NY: Crabtree Publishing Company, 2023.

Colson, Rob. *Asia*. Buffalo, NY: Enslow Publishing, 2025.

London, Martha. *Asia*. Lake Elmo, MN: Focus Readers, 2021.

Websites

BBC Bitesize: Let's Explore Asia
www.bbc.co.uk/bitesize/articles/zmy7m39
This website offers fun facts about Asia, as well as videos, activities, and a quiz.

***National Geographic*: Philippines Photos**
www.nationalgeographic.com/travel/article/philippines-photos
This photo gallery shows the people, places, and natural wonders that you can find in the Philippines.

***National Geographic Kids*: China Country Profile**
Kids.nationalgeographic.com/geography/countries/article/china
National Geographic Kids breaks down the basics of Chinese geography, culture, and more.

INDEX